What If We Do
NOTHING?

DRUG TRAFFICKING

Nathaniel Harris

Gareth Stevens
Publishing

Please visit our web site at: www.garethstevens.com.
For a free color catalog describing Gareth Stevens Publishing's list of high-quality books, call 1-800-542-2595 (USA) or 1-800-387-3178 (Canada). Gareth Stevens Publishing's fax: 1-877-542-2596.

Library of Congress Cataloging-in-Publication Data

Harris, Nathaniel, 1937-
    Drug trafficking / by Nathaniel Harris.
      p. cm. – (What if we do nothing?)
    Includes bibliographical references and index.
    ISBN-10: 1-4339-1981-8   ISBN-13: 978-1-4339-1981-7 (lib. bdg.)
    1. Drug traffic. 2. Drugs. I. Title.
HV5801.H358   2010
363.45–dc22   2008052495

This North American edition published in 2010 by Gareth Stevens Publishing under license from Arcturus Publishing Limited.
Gareth Stevens Publishing
A Weekly Reader® Company
1 Reader's Digest Road
Pleasantville, NY 10570-7000 USA

Copyright © 2009 Arcturus Publishing Limited
Produced by Arcturus Publishing Limited
26/27 Bickels Yard, 151-153 Bermondsey Street, London SE1 3HA

Series Concept: Alex Woolf
Editor: Alex Woolf
Designer: Phipps Design
Picture Researcher: Alex Woolf

Gareth Stevens Executive Managing Editor: Lisa M. Herrington
Gareth Stevens Editors: Jayne Keedle, Joann Jovinelly
Gareth Stevens Senior Designer: Keith Plechaty

Picture Credits: Corbis: Cover, bottom left (Bob Thomas), cover, top right (Reuters), 5 (Bob Thomas), 6 (Scott Houston/Sygma), 9 (Ed Kashi), 13 (Reuters), 14 (John and Lisa Merrill), 16 (Andy Clark/Reuters), 24 (Oswaldo Rivas/Reuters), 28 (Gideon Mendel for The International HIV/AIDS Alliance), 31 (Bettmann), 35 (Adrees Latif/Reuters), 36 (Reuters), 39 (Damir Sagolj/Reuters), 40 (David Bathgate), 42 (Reuters), 44 (Scott Houston); Getty Images: 10 (Paula Bronstein), 21 (Robert Nickelsberg), 22 (Rodrigo Arangua/AFP), 33 (Santi Visalli, Inc.); PA Photos: 17 (AP); Rex Features: 18 (Sam Foot); Science Photo Library: 27 (CC Studio); Shutterstock: Cover, background (Ricardo A. Alves).

Cover pictures: Bottom left: A young drug addict sits on the floor of a public toilet. Top right: Pakistani anti-narcotics police display bags of heroin and morphine seized from Iranian drug smugglers in Turbat, near the Iranian border, in 2002. Background: A poppy field. Opium, as well as opiates such as morphine and heroin, are processed from the sap of the opium poppy.

Every attempt has been made to clear copyright. Should there be any inadvertent omission, please apply to the publisher for rectification.

Printed in the United States

1 2 3 4 5 6 7 8 9 15 14 13 12 11 10 09

Contents

CHAPTER 1

The Trouble With Drugs

It is 2025. Tom and his friends occupy an abandoned house. They don't do much of anything. Mostly they talk about drugs and how to get a steady supply of them. "No problem," says Tom. "There are dealers everywhere. You can buy as much as you want. The problem is finding the money for them." That's hard, especially when you need to take more and more drugs just to keep from feeling bad. Tom's friends also talk about Julie, a girl who recently died from a drug overdose. Tom considers his friends. They aren't healthy, and neither is he. Then, another friend turns up with some drugs. There is just about enough to go round. One after another, the friends inject the drug into their veins. Soon, for a little while, they will be "high" and won't care what happens to them.

Victims of a Global Trade

The future doesn't look good for those young drug addicts. Illegal drug use is spoiling their lives. Even if you think that their drug abuse problem is their own fault, they need help. If they want to stop, they will find it nearly impossible to do so on their own. It seems drugs are everywhere. Even now, well before 2025, producing and supplying illegal drugs is big business. "Trafficking" means illegal trading, and drug trafficking is a criminal activity on an international scale. It involves many thousands of people.

This diagram shows estimated world drug use among people in the age group 15-64. The total age group numbers around 4,117 million. Of those, around 220 million use drugs. Problem drug users (defined by the United Nations as people who inject a drug or make regular or long-term use of opium-based drugs, cocaine, or amphetamines) number around 30 million.

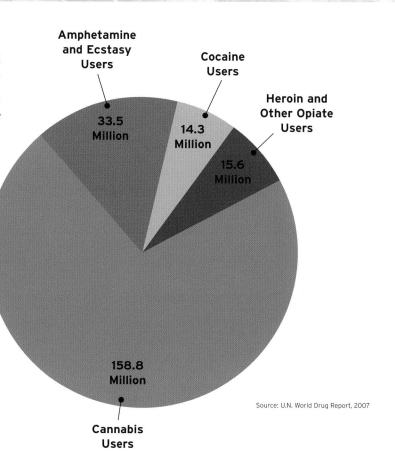

Amphetamine and Ecstasy Users — 33.5 Million

Cocaine Users — 14.3 Million

Heroin and Other Opiate Users — 15.6 Million

Cannabis Users — 158.8 Million

Source: U.N. World Drug Report, 2007

What Are Drugs?

Drugs are chemical substances that often have a pleasurable physical or mental effect. Taking drugs can influence the way people feel or think, or the way their bodies work. When we talk about drugs as a problem or menace, we are actually talking about illegal drugs, or narcotics. We often use the word drugs as shorthand for illegal drugs, but we should remember that there are legal as well as illegal drugs. Medicines are also called drugs. In fact, some illegal drugs were originally developed as medicines. They were only outlawed, or prescribed and sold under strictly controlled conditions, when experts realized that they might be abused. Other, non-medicinal drugs are legally sold and used every day. Those include alcohol, the nicotine in tobacco, and the caffeine in coffee, tea, and soft drinks.

A young addict has lost almost everything. He is homeless and has nothing left except some drug-taking gear and a mattress. Not every drug abuser ends up homeless, but taking illegal drugs can easily ruin a person's life.

Types of Drugs

Drugs can be divided into several groups. Each group has widely different effects. One group consists of stimulants. Those energizing drugs increase the heart rate. Thoughts race through the mind. People who have taken stimulants may act strangely or grind their teeth. In some cases, they suffer from serious mental disorders. Stimulants include cocaine, amphetamines, crystal meth (methamphetamine), and ecstasy.

Another drug group, called depressants, have the opposite effect. They decrease the heart rate and brain function. Users of depressants or sedatives usually feel extremely relaxed, numb, tired, or even

A young man has a good time at a New York nightclub, showing off with glow sticks. In the 1990s, ecstasy became the club-goers drug of choice, energizing users so that they could dance all night long.

uncoordinated. Opium, heroin, and most forms of cannabis (marijuana and hashish) are depressants.

The third drug group consists of hallucinogens. Those are drugs that make users hallucinate, which means that they experience reality in an abnormal way. The drug user may see everything in intensely vivid colors or mistake imaginary things for realities. One type of hallucinogen is the synthetic (human-made) drug LSD (lysergic acid diethylamide). Another is "magic mushrooms", which describes two species of wild mushrooms, liberty cap and fly agaric.

Drug Dangers

Drugs interfere with the normal way the mind and body work, so it is no great surprise that there are disadvantages to drug abuse. One risk is that drug users might take an overdose — a dangerously large amount of a drug. An overdose is almost always very serious, and sometimes fatal. It can happen because the drug user is careless or badly informed. It can also happen because the ingredients of illegal substances are not officially checked and are dangerous. For example, the proportions of the drug and other ingredients it may be mixed with may be wrong. Pure heroin and pure cocaine are killers. They need to be combined with other substances before they are taken. Sometimes the substances added those drugs may also be hazardous.

LEGAL, BUT LETHAL

In most societies, adults can legally buy and use alcohol and tobacco. For a long time, those drugs were considered a normal part of life. Many people still think of them in that way, yet both drugs cause illness and death. In the United States, the cost of alcohol abuse in terms of medical treatment, policing, and lost working days in 2007 was estimated at $185 billion. The links between smoking and diseases such as cancer are also well established. Smoking has declined in the United States, yet smoking-related healthcare and other costs related to respiratory illnesses were estimated at $167 billion in 2005.

Drug taking has many other dangers. Just as drugs differ from one another, so do their risks. Side effects and after effects can include sweating, a dry mouth, vomiting, constipation, and diarrhea. More unpleasant things can happen while the user is under the influence of the drug. Some people suffer panic attacks. Hallucinogenic drugs can cause a "bad trip" in which the user experiences imaginary horrors and behaves irrationally. The Netherlands is generally less tough on drugs than most of its European neighbors, but in 2007 it banned the sale of hallucinogenic mushrooms after users behaved strangely or violently. In one incident, a girl died.

Opposite: A woman gets comforted in a hospital in San Francisco, California. She is suffering from symptoms of withdrawal. Her body craves the drug to which she has become addicted.

Addiction

One major problem with many drugs is that highs are typically followed by lows. When the effect of the drug wears off, the user is often left feeling tired, depressed, or even irritable. He or she may take the drug again in order to feel better. That is one way in which people slip from occasional drug use into addiction or drug dependence. Addicts are people who need to take a drug frequently and cannot stop, even when they realize that taking drugs is ruining their lives.

Most drugs are addictive to a greater or lesser extent. Users of a drug such as heroin eventually need it as a relief rather than a pleasure. They suffer from terrible physical pain when they cannot get it or are trying to give it up. Other drugs are described as only psychologically addictive. They cause addiction through their influence on the mind. To stop taking them may not be physically uncomfortable, but the user's brain craves the release given by the drug and the way it enables them to avoid any problems and anxieties they experience in their life.

HEROIN

Heroin is generally regarded as the most dangerous of all illegal drugs. It is an opiate – one of a range of drugs made from the opium poppy, including opium, morphine, and codeine. Heroin was originally developed around 1900 as an exceptionally powerful painkiller. Illegally sold in powder form, it can be sniffed or smoked. Many users inject it into a vein to achieve a more intense "high". Heroin is highly addictive and causes a number of ailments. It also carries more serious health risks from overdosing, collapsed veins, and diseases caught through sharing needles, such as HIV/AIDS and hepatitis C.

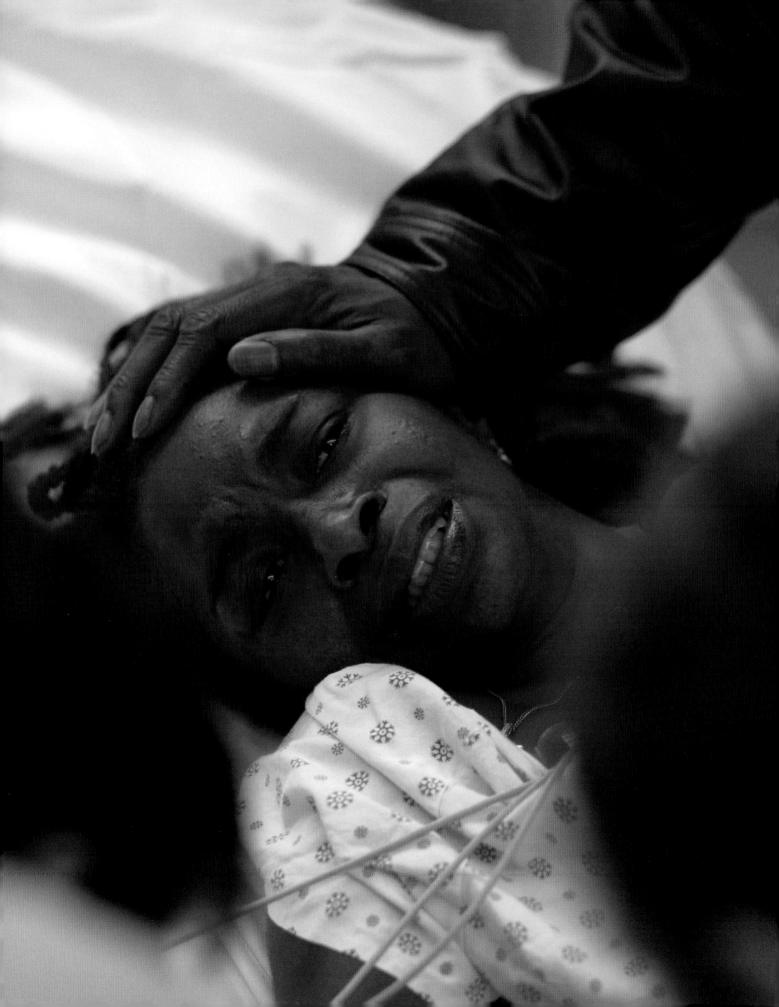

Addicts take large amounts of their drug. Their systems get used to it, and they eventually need more and more of the drug to achieve the same effect. Even if they can afford to buy large quantities, addicts find that the drug dominates their lives and prevents them from having normal relationships. Furthermore, taking large quantities of a drug makes its long-term effects worse. Addicts suffer serious mental problems or a failure of the heart or liver. Regular snorting of cocaine has a particularly unattractive effect: It destroys the snorter's septum, the partition separating the nostrils. Those who

A boy inhales glue from a bag on the streets of Kathmandu, Nepal. Children in many countries find it easy to obtain everyday products that can be used as drugs.

take more than one type of drug at a time are even more likely to develop serious health problems.

All Types of People Take Drugs

Despite the risks, all types of people from all over the world use drugs. The drug taker is often portrayed as a young person, because the young are typically rebellious and like to take risks. Young people also sometimes find it hard to resist peer pressure — the pressure to behave like other young people they know.

Antidrug advocates target the young, hoping to prevent them from starting a drug habit. But millions of adults are also users. They belong to all sorts of groups, ranging from cocaine-snorting businesspeople and partygoers to poor people, who take drugs to forget their troubles. Sports enthusiasts sometimes use drugs called steroids to buildup muscles and improve athletic performance.

Not all drug users are supplied by dealers. Some adults who use prescription drugs become addicted to them. And many children obtain legally available solvents, such as glue, and get a high from sniffing them.

People have used drugs for thousands of years. But in modern times, mass production, rapid communication, and international transportation have made large quantities of drugs available all over the world.

Sending a Message

Research has identified many of the dangers of drug taking, but many people — including smokers and drinkers — ignore those messages. Governments see it as their duty to protect citizens and make sure that society is not disrupted by drug taking. It penalizes drug users and imposes even harsher penalties on those who supply and profit from illegal drugs — the traffickers.

WHAT WOULD YOU DO?

You Are in Charge

You are an outstanding sports player, greatly admired by young people. You are invited to take part in an antidrug TV advertising campaign. Do you:

■ refuse, perhaps because you fear that young people will see you as a lecturing adult instead of a hero?

■ accept, and be ready to speak out about avoiding all drugs?

■ accept, but insist on talking mainly about the drugs used in professional sports?

CHAPTER 2

Trafficking Across Frontiers

It is 2025. Rosalia is a poor farmer's daughter, just 13 years old. Civil wars and violent changes of government have wrecked the South American country where she lives. The poor are starving and must do whatever they can to survive. Soldiers have targeted her family's farm. They have arrested Rosalia's father and brothers and have destroyed their illegal coca crop, which outsiders buy and use to make cocaine. Rosalia's mother is too upset to think about the future, and Rosalia wonders how they will survive. All they can do is work the land — but what can they grow? Rosalia would like to be respectable and grow oranges or coffee, but those crops bring in hardly any money. She fears that her family will have no choice but to grow a new coca crop and hope the soldiers will stay away.

Government Action

Most countries have made laws that penalize people who produce, supply, or use illegal drugs. But drug trafficking is not just a national problem — it is international, because many of the drugs are smuggled from country to country. A nation's customs officers, often assisted by police, try to locate drugs that are being smuggled across its borders. Customs officials will confiscate the drugs and arrest the offenders. Law enforcement agencies from different nations work together with international organizations, such as the United Nations and the international police agency, Interpol, to stop drug trafficking.

A Global Business

Both national and international agencies face difficult problems. Huge profits can be made from international drug trafficking. That means traffickers can afford to organize their operations to continue to prosper even if authorities seize large quantities of their smuggled drugs. Many of the drugs they handle are transported across continents to reach profitable markets in wealthy parts of the world such as North America, Europe, and Australia.

THE PRESIDENT'S LIST

Every year the U.S. president sends a list of countries to Congress. Those are countries identified as major producers of illegal drugs or major drug-transit countries, or countries through which drugs pass. In 2008, the list named the following countries:

- Afghanistan
- The Bahamas
- Bolivia
- Brazil
- Burma
- Colombia
- Dominican Republic

- Ecuador
- Guatemala
- Haiti
- India
- Jamaica
- Laos
- Mexico

- Nigeria
- Pakistan
- Panama
- Paraguay
- Peru
- Venezuela

Policemen carry packs of cocaine obtained during a drug bust in Buenaventura, Colombia. The drug cache is one part of a 6,614-pound (3,000-kilogram) haul that was seized. If law enforcement had not acted, the drugs would have been smuggled into Mexico, probably bound for drug dealers in the United States.

COCAINE AND CRACK

Cocaine was developed in the 1850s. Its main ingredient is a substance extracted from the leaves of the South American coca plant. For thousands of years, South American mountain peoples chewed dried coca leaves, which acted as a mild, natural stimulant. Cocaine is much more powerful. It is usually sold as a white powder and is commonly snorted. Crack, another form of cocaine, is smoked. Using cocaine or crack causes violent mood swings. Both drugs are highly addictive. Users of either drug are at risk for serious health problems. Heavy use of crack, for example, can cause mental illness.

A Peruvian farmer chews a coca leaf. Coca has long been used by people in the mountainous regions of South America. Unlike the hard drugs cocaine and crack, the natural coca leaf produces a mild stimulative effect.

Smuggling Heroin and Cocaine

Heroin comes from opium poppies grown in Afghanistan and other Asian countries. In South American countries such as Colombia and Bolivia, coca leaves are processed to make cocaine and crack. Typically, cocaine is smuggled from Colombia into the United States through Mexico, and into European countries via West Africa.

The growers of opium poppies and coca plants are not hardened criminals. They are mostly poor farmers who struggle to survive. They are not paid large amounts of money for their crops, although the drugs made from them will eventually command high prices on city streets. The farmers would probably prefer to grow legal crops, but only the traffickers will pay prices that enable them to survive.

MARIJUANA

Marijuana comes from the cannabis plant. It is used by almost 160 million people and is the most popular illegal drug in the world. Cannabis is grown in at least 172 countries and sold in the form of leaves or a dark, dried resin called hashish. Marijuana is normally smoked, but it can also be mixed with food and eaten. Except in its very strongest form, the drug has a relaxing effect, rendering users dreamy and inactive. Although some people view marijuana as a relatively harmless drug, studies show it can have long-term effects on the brain and may cause cancer. The U.S. government regards it as a "gateway" drug, meaning that it may encourage users to try harder drugs.

Smuggling Marijuana

Unlike heroin and cocaine, cannabis can be grown in many parts of the world. Marijuana leaves are bulkier than many other drugs, but nevertheless they are widely smuggled. Cannabis grown illegally in the United States may be smuggled across state borders. Cannabis is typically smuggled into the United States from Mexico and Canada. The long U.S. borders are hard to police. Although large quantities of marijuana are seized every year, substantial amounts get through.

Smuggling Laboratory Drugs

Drugs made in the laboratory, such as amphetamines, crystal meth, and LSD, are also smuggled into many states. Traffickers may set up illicit, or illegal, laboratories in the country where they intend to sell the drugs, avoiding the risks involved in smuggling. But many of the traffickers prefer to manufacture the drugs in countries where policing is weak or penalties are relatively light. They employ other people to do the smuggling across borders, to minimize the risks they take themselves.

Smuggling Methods

Drug smugglers employ a variety of methods. Where there are remote areas to be crossed, or the borders are poorly policed, vehicles or planes may transport large quantities of drugs with little danger of being caught. The smugglers may well be professional criminals, prepared to use violence if they meet with opposition.

A Canadian police officer displays a fake duck egg packed with heroin, a part of a large consignment of heroin and ecstasy. Ingeniously, smugglers hid the drugs inside and among preserved duck eggs that had been shipped from China to Canada.

LABORATORY DRUGS

The main ingredients of many drugs come from plants. Heroin, cocaine, hallucinogenic mushrooms, and marijuana are all plant-based drugs, though they may be processed in a laboratory before they are sold. But there are also synthetic (human-made) drugs made entirely in laboratories, using chemicals. Those include powerful stimulants, such as amphetamines ("speed"), ecstasy, and methamphetamine ("crystal meth"). Crystal meth is a concentrated and particularly dangerous form of amphetamine. It is highly additive and has been widely used in the United States, Australia, and New Zealand since the 1990s.

The best-known laboratory-made hallucinogen is LSD, which was highly popular in the 1960s and 1970s. Laboratory drugs are hard for the police to trace, since they can be made close to the area where they are sold, unlike drugs that have to be smuggled across borders.

In areas where border controls operate more effectively, smugglers attempt all sorts of ingenious ways to conceal their cargo or bluff their way through customs. For example, they may use official vehicles or stow the drugs in hidden compartments in the bodywork of cars or trucks. If the smugglers succeed, they get through with large quantities of the drug. However, the risk of detection is great. Well-trained security forces are on the job, backed by expert assistants such as a team of dogs who are trained to identify drugs by their smells!

These puppies were rescued from a Colombian laboratory. Drug traffickers were intending to surgically implant the dogs with packets of liquid heroin and carry them into the United States.

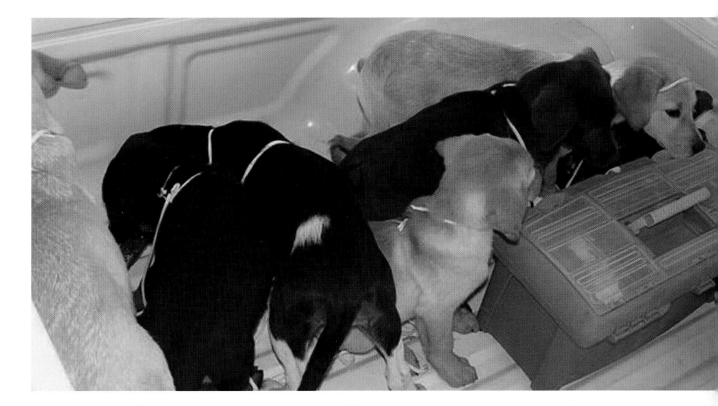

Mules

An alternative way in which smugglers operate is to use "mules". Those are individuals who bring drugs into a country by carrying them on, or inside, their bodies. Usually the mule is not a professional criminal but an ordinary person who is desperately poor, in trouble, or foolishly tempted by the prospect of quick and easy money. Mules hope that, since they appear to be ordinary travelers or tourists, they will pass through busy customs points unchecked.

Mules may be carrying drugs in a pocket or backpack. A more cunning but extremely dangerous option is to swallow packets of the drugs. They are sealed in latex or a similar material and carried across the border hidden in the mule's body. Authorities have become aware of this trick, however, and mules who use this method may well be caught and end up in prison. In some countries, drug mules face very harsh penalties, including the death sentence.

An even greater danger is that the wrapping will burst open. If that happens, a large quantity of the drug will be released into the mule's system, probably with fatal results. Drug trafficking across frontiers is a business in which the people at the top make fortunes and those at the bottom take the risks.

Distribution

The drugs that come onto the market in a particular country may have been produced there or may have been smuggled in from abroad. In both cases, the criminals' next step is to distribute the

This dramatized photo shows a young man buying drugs from a dealer. In reality, the deal would have been done less openly, probably behind closed doors.

drugs. Large quantities are broken up into smaller amounts. Those pass through the hands of a succession of traffickers. Eventually, most of the supply reaches local dealers who sell the drugs directly to the people who want to use them.

Dealers

The dealers are often drug users, too. Many sell drugs to finance their own addiction or habit. They may try to make contacts or even sell drugs on the street, looking for new customers in places such as schools and youth centers. Once they have built up regular contacts, they may start to carry out transactions in their own homes. In either case, the drug dealers' activities tend to become widely known in the local area, making it more likely that the police will investigate sooner or later and arrest them.

WHAT WOULD YOU DO?

You Are in Charge
You are the leader of a country in which farmers find it hard to make a living except by growing illegal crops for drug production. Which solution seems most helpful?

■ Find the illegal crops, destroy them, and arrest the farmers.

■ Patrol your country's borders more thoroughly, cooperating with neighboring countries to stop the drugs from reaching their intended markets.

■ Encourage farmers to cultivate legal crops by providing irrigation and financial help to buy seeds, fertilizers, and new equipment.

■ Reward farmers who grow legal food crops by paying them for each harvest brought in, or by guaranteeing a reasonable price for produce?

CHAPTER 3

Drugs and Crime

It is 2025. During a hot summer day, Josh and his friends are sitting outside the house, trying to keep cool. They talk about the vicious gang wars that are terrorizing the city. With so much money to be made from drug dealing, the gangs are constantly fighting over territory. Anybody who happens to be at the scene is likely to get hurt. During the conversation, a car passes, shots ring out, and the car speeds away. Two men on the other side of the street fall to the ground, bleeding. They are probably involved in gang warfare. But one of the shots has also hit a little girl who was playing nearby. When Josh and his friends reach her, she is already dead. Crossfire killing among gang members happens so frequently that it is unlikely even to get a mention on the evening news.

Gangs

People who become drug traffickers are committing crimes, whether they make, move, or sell illegal substances. In most countries, users of drugs are also breaking the law. But as well as those obvious illegalities, there are many other important links between drugs and crime.

In a number of U.S. cities, the selling of drugs has been taken over by armed gangs. In some cities, gangs dominate entire neighborhoods, usually in the poorest areas. The power of the gangs makes it difficult for the police to investigate crimes or find witnesses brave enough to provide evidence about illegal activities.

Challenges to a dominant gang are most likely to come from rival gangs. The rival gangs compete for areas of a city they aim to supply with drugs. Those gangs then control the drug supply in those areas. Expanding their territory brings power, income, and prestige. Vicious gang wars are fought over who rules a particular area or "turf". It is not yet 2025, but killings are already common in most large cities. They often take the form of drive-by shootings in which one or more members of a rival gang are shot down by gunmen from a passing car. Innocent bystanders are often hit and killed.

Opposite: **A police officer takes no chances when questioning drug suspects, making them rest their hands on a car so they cannot reach for any weapons. The young men were linked with a violent drug-dealing gang. Marijuana was found in their car.**

CRIMINAL PROFITS FROM DRUG SALES

Criminal gangs make huge profits from drug trafficking. The statistics below show the price of heroin at each stage of its journey from Asia to the United Kingdom, along with the percentage markup (the percentage increase in the price charged at each stage).

	Value	Markup
Price per kilo (2.2 pounds) paid to the farmer	$637	
Price per kilo paid to Turkish handlers	$11,535	1800%
Price per kilo paid on entering the United Kingdom	$29,010	151%
Price per kilo for which the drug is sold on the street*	$73,122	69%

*Individual street sales will be for much smaller amounts than a kilo. Cost in dollars converted from U.K. pounds based on exchange rates as of March 2009.

Source: *Understanding Drug Markets and How to Influence Them* (Beckley Foundation Policy Program, 2008)

Gang violence of this kind is most common in the United States, but in recent years it has begun to appear in other countries, notably South Africa. Gun crime has also increased in the United Kingdom and is strongly linked to drugs. In cities such as Liverpool, Birmingham, and London, several people have been killed by stray bullets during battles between gangs.

Drug Barons

Street dealers and gangsters take many risks. The criminals at the top of trafficking organizations make the most money and have the best chance of escaping arrest. Even when their identities are known, it is not easy to trace crimes back to those "drug barons" and convict them for their crimes. Some drug barons, like Pablo Escobar (page 36), are notorious gang figures. Others remain unknown. In 2007, police raided a Mexico City pharmaceutical company and the home of its president. The police found evidence that the company was a front for drug trafficking. The seemingly respectable president was the leader in charge of the operation. Police confiscated a record-breaking $207 million, all in cash, from the president's home.

Luiz Fernando da Costa is being taken back to his native Brazil in 2001 after being captured during a gun battle in Colombia. Once back home, he was convicted of drug trafficking and imprisoned.

Unusual Suspects

Drugs are linked to crime in many ways. The massive profits made from drug trafficking lure some unlikely people into a life of crime. Law enforcement officers have been caught smuggling drugs, as have struggling business owners. In some countries, terrorists and revolutionaries finance their activities through drug trafficking or by demanding payments from farmers who grow drug crops.

Funding a Habit

Drug users break the law when they take drugs, but they are also likely to commit other crimes. Most people who become heavy drug users do not have the large amounts of money required to afford all the drugs they use. They commit crimes to obtain money to fund their drug habits, or because drug use has kept them so poor that they steal in order to live. In one survey, 9 out of 10 heroin and crack users claimed that they had committed crimes to pay for their drugs. Shoplifting, burglary, mugging, and car theft are all typical drug-related crimes. Some users commit crimes while under the influence of drugs, such as those who drive while on drugs and cause accidents. Statistics show that more than half a million people in U.S. prisons have been sent there for drug offenses. Still more have been incarcerated for drug-related crimes.

WHAT WOULD YOU DO?

You Are in Charge

You have been appointed by the government to create a policy on drugs and drug-related crime within your country. Better results are badly needed. Do you:

- Push for more resources and greater police power to search premises and arrest and hold suspects.

- Use available resources to target only the most dangerous drug users.

- Promote educational programs that highlight the dangers and drawbacks of drug use.

- Improve programs to rehabilitate addicts to help them end their addiction.

- Allow addicts who commit crimes to join drug rehabilitation and education programs instead of sending them to prison.

CHAPTER 4

The Social Cost

It is 2025. Natasha is a drug addict who has engaged in reckless behavior because of her habit. She has hepatitis C, a disease that she caught by sharing the needles of hypodermic syringes with fellow addicts. She realizes that drug use is ruining her life. But in 2025, the hospital system can no longer cope with the burden of caring for drug addicts. Natasha has no prospect of treatment for her addiction, or even for the disease that is damaging her liver. She tries to stop taking drugs, but she lacks social support. She has long ago lost touch with her family, who might have helped her get sober. Since all of her friends are drug users, her recovery seems unlikely.

Damaged Lives

Drug trafficking and illegal drug use have harmful effects on society at many levels. The impact on the users is obvious. Heavy users and addicts are unhealthy and to have shorter lives than nonusers. If they are young, they may fail to complete their studies. They often lose their jobs and they are unlikely to make the best of their talents or achieve their career goals. Drug addicts frequently damage or destroy their relationships with the people closest to them — their parents, spouses, children, friends, and work colleagues. If their need for drugs drives them to commit crimes, they will probably end up in prison or even dead.

A drug addict smokes crack in a run-down house in Managua, Nicaragua. Drug problems damage countries and people, whether they are rich or poor. Drugs have fueled gang violence and wars in Central America.

Family Breakdown

Family and friends often do their best to help someone close to them overcome a drug problem. However, drug use can affect their lives, too. A user may become violent or steal from the family to buy drugs. Even if that does not happen, the user's mood swings and erratic lifestyle put terrible strains on family relationships. Those relationships often break down, leaving members devastated. The user often leaves the family, losing contact with everybody and moving mainly among fellow users, making it unlikely that he or she will ever break his or her drug habit.

THE MOST DANGEROUS DRUGS

Research published in the British medical journal *The Lancet* listed the most dangerous drugs. The ratings are based on harm to the user, likelihood of becoming addicted, and harm to society. Starting with the worst, the first 12 out of 20 were:

1.	Heroin	a highly-addictive depressant
2.	Cocaine	a highly-addictive stimulant
3.	Barbiturates	a range of drugs with powerfully depressant effects
4.	Methadone	a drug used to treat drug addiction, but also sold on the street as an illegal drug
5.	Alcohol	a legal drug found in liquors, wines, and beers
6.	Ketamine	a powerful depressant that causes loss of body sensation
7.	Benzodiazepines	a range of drugs that can be used to treat drug highs that get out of hand, but are highly addictive
8.	Amphetamines	human-made stimulants
9.	Tobacco	a legal drug found in cigarettes
10.	Buprenorphine	a painkiller abused by drug takers
11.	Cannabis	a natural, but illegal, depressant
12.	Solvents	chemical substances that are harmful when inhaled

Two legal drugs are high on the list: **alcohol** (no. 5) and **tobacco** (no. 9). Some well-known illegal drugs came lower down the list, notably **LSD** (no. 14) and **ecstasy** (no. 18).

Damage to Society

Illegal drugs affect the lives of individuals, but they also have a powerful effect on society as a whole. Governments spend huge sums trying to suppress drug taking and trafficking. Dealing with the health and social problems caused by drug users is also a major expense. Social service agencies may become involved when drug users cannot cope with everyday life or when their families or children need to be helped or even removed from the home and taken into foster care. Governments pay for those social costs of drugs with citizens' taxes. Experts in various countries have estimated the social costs of illegal drugs at billions of dollars.

SOCIAL COSTS OF ILLEGAL DRUGS

These are some recent estimates of the total social cost of illegal drug use on some nations. All figures are in billions of U.S. dollars.

Country	Year	Amount
United States	2002	$180.9
United Kingdom	2008	$28.4
Canada	2002	$8.2
Australia	2005	$8.1
New Zealand	2006	$1.3

Sources: The Economic Costs of Drug Abuse in the United States 1992-2002 (2004); The Financial Cost of Addiction (Addaction, 2008); The Cost of Substance Abuse in Canada 2002 (2006); The Costs of Tobacco, Alcohol and Illicit Drug Abuse to Australian Society in 2004/5; Research by Business and Economic Research, Ltd. for the New Zealand Police (2008)

The Cost of Crime

For most countries, crime is the largest of all social costs. The high number of drug-related crimes mean that governments must spend very large sums on law enforcement, the justice system, prisons, and the large numbers of people and institutions linked with them. In 2007, there were 1.8 million arrests in the United States for drug offenses. At the end of 2008, as many as 2.3 million people were in prison in the United States, many for drug-related crimes.

Health Costs

The health costs of drug use are also extremely substantial. Health services must:

- Deal with medical emergencies caused by drug overdoses and drug-related accidents
- Provide treatment for a range of illnesses associated with drug use, including mental problems
- Offer expensive medicines to treat infections spread by sharing needles, or pay for programs that offer clean needles to addicts
- Provide for the special health needs of pregnant addicts and their children
- Operate programs to help people overcome their addictions

Needles and Disease

Many addicts inject drugs like heroin straight into their veins, using hypodermic syringes. Not being medically trained, they may damage themselves or contract infections such as blood poisoning. An even more dangerous practice is for several users to share the same needle. Any infection in one user's blood, such as hepatitis C, can be passed on to the others.

In this dramatized photograph, a woman is using legally prescribed drugs to get high. Those pills are just as dangerous as illegal drugs, especially if they are not used as directed by a physican. Prescription drug abuse is a growing problem. In this example, the woman is taking prescription pills with alcohol, a potentially deadly combination.

Very serious diseases, such as human immunodeficiency virus (HIV) and hepatitis C, can be caught in this way. Hepatitis C attacks the liver and can kill. The HIV virus destroys the immune system, which protects the body against infections. As a result, HIV can lead on to acquired immunodeficiency syndrome (AIDS), a life-threatening condition. HIV is most commonly contracted through sexual activity, but needle-sharing has claimed many additional victims.

Economic Costs

In addition to those huge social expenses, there are costs to the economy. Those costs are hard to calculate because they mostly take the form of lost income or inefficiency in many offices and other workplaces. Heavy drug users tend to be unreliable and unhealthy workers, which makes their places of employment less productive. The users' health problems will cause them to be sick and absent more often than typical employees.

A young drug addict in Kiev, Ukraine, is preparing to inject herself. Like many people who inject drugs, she became HIV-positive through sharing needles. Given help, she stopped sharing and began to distribute clean needles and syringes to other users to try to prevent the spread of disease.

If users become desperate for money to pay for the drugs they take, they may steal from their employers or their fellow workers. Such thefts create an atmosphere of distrust until the culprit is discovered, and may have long-lasting effects on work relationships. Whether drug users are sick, inefficient, or commit crimes, they will probably lose their jobs and will find it harder and harder to get new ones. Instead of contributing to society, they will become a burden on it.

All resources are limited. The money spent on drug-related crime, health, and work problems cannot be spent on other things. Those problems cost society billions of dollars. The U.S. response has been to declare a "War on Drugs" — an attempt to stamp out drug use and drug trafficking.

WHAT WOULD YOU DO?

You Are in Charge

You work for the government's department of health. More and more cases of a serious disease are appearing. You need to educate people about the disease and treat those who have it. The disease can be caught in various ways but some sufferers have contracted it through drug use, by sharing the needles with which they inject themselves. You have limited resources. Will you:

- focus on reaching people who don't use drugs? Drug users have themselves to blame if they get the disease.

- make a special effort to reach drug users because they are likely to spread the disease to others?

- provide drug addicts with sterile needles to try to prevent the disease from spreading?

- offer free treatment to drug users if they agree to enter rehabilitation programs and stop using drugs?

CHAPTER 5

Fighting the Traffickers

It is 2025. Charlie is a guard who belongs to a unit that patrols U.S. borders to stop people from entering the country illegally. That task has become almost impossible. United States' borders are being crossed all along their lengths. Many intruders are carrying illegal drugs. Neighboring countries are close to collapse and can do nothing about drug trafficking. Because it is so profitable, the traffickers are able to arm themselves at least as well as the border guards, whose job has become increasingly dangerous. Charlie is a brave man, but he worries about what will become of his wife and children if he is killed. Then the news breaks. A heavily armed party of traffickers has been spotted 50 miles (80 km) away, heading for the border at breakneck speed. There is no time to arrange for backup. Charlie and the rest of the unit prepare to stop the border-crossers in their tracks.

Changing Attitudes

Drug use has a long history, but laws against using drugs are comparatively recent. During the 1800s, drugs were freely available in countries like Britain and the United States. Opium was widely used as a painkiller and could be bought over the counter in pharmacies. Laudanum, a liquid form of the drug (mixed with alcohol), was especially popular. A number of people, including some famous writers, began taking laudanum as medicine and eventually became addicted to it.

Nineteenth-century chemists made many discoveries that led to the manufacture of stronger drugs. Opium was developed into morphine in 1803, and morphine into heroin in 1898. In 1874, cocaine was extracted from coca leaves. At first those drugs were hailed as great scientific achievements. For a time cocaine was even used as an ingredient in Coca-Cola. Later, scientists became aware that drugs such as heroin and cocaine were unsuitable for medical use. They also realized that the supply of even medically beneficial drugs such as morphine needed to be controlled.

CHINA AND OPIUM

During the 1800s, China developed a serious drug problem. Opium consumption increased steadily as supplies of the drug arrived from India, which was then under British rule. When China tried to ban opium, the British fought two wars in 1839–1842 and 1856–1860 that forced the Chinese government to allow opium into the country. Later, Chinese immigrants brought the habit to the United Kingdom and the United States. The opium dens in which they smoked the drug gained a bad reputation. Previously the victims of the opium trade, the Chinese were now blamed for bringing the highly addictive drug to the West.

This photograph of drug users in an opium den in Chinatown, the part of New York where most Chinese once lived, was taken in 1925. Images like this one fed people's prejudices and made it easy for them to believe that the Chinese were to blame for U.S. drug problems.

Antidrug Legislation

Fear and concern about Chinese opium dens led to the first U.S. antidrug laws, which were passed by the city of San Francisco in 1875. In 1909, the United States took the first international action against the opium trade. A U.S.-sponsored meeting led to the Hague Convention in 1912. That was an international agreement that committed members to outlaw opium. In 1914, the United States passed the Harrison Narcotic Act, the first federal antidrug law. In 1920, the British government also took action, passing the Dangerous Drugs Act.

Those early measures became the basis for many later national and international laws to ban recreational drug use. Lists of illegal drugs became steadily longer as their dangers were fully realized. However, in some cases this recognition came surprisingly late. Amphetamines, though manufactured since 1887, were still frequently issued to troops during World War II (1939–1945) to combat battle fatigue. Amphetamines only became illegal in the United States and the United Kingdom in the mid-1960s. Similarly, ecstasy was freely available until the mid-1980s.

Early alarms over cocaine and heroin gave way to other concerns. For a long time, attention in the United States focused on alcohol, which was an illegal drug from 1919 until 1933 (the Prohibition era). Then the emphasis shifted to marijuana, which Congress effectively outlawed in 1937 and penalized increasingly harshly in the 1950s. In the United States cannabis was, and is, regarded as being as dangerous as cocaine and heroin.

In the 1960s, drug taking became an important part of the youth culture that developed in the United States, the United Kingdom, and many other countries. Governments grew alarmed enough to introduce new antidrug laws. The United Kingdom passed

PROHIBITION

In 1920, whiskey, beer, and all other alcoholic drinks were banned in the United States. That period in American history is known as Prohibition. Millions of Americans still wanted to drink, so the import, manufacture, and sale of liquor was taken over by criminals. Huge profits were at stake and vicious gang wars broke out for control of the trade. Corruption was widespread, including bribery of police officers. Ordinary people became law-breakers, buying alcohol from dealers or visiting "speakeasies" (underground clubs that sold alcoholic drinks). Prohibition ended in 1933, and is today considered a failed policy.

This 1968 photograph of a man in face paint, a mock uniform, and a wide grin conveys the carefree spirit of many young people in the 1960s. The painted card on his hat reads LSD — the name of the most popular hallucinogenic drug of the period.

the Misuse of Drugs Act (1971), which combined and updated earlier laws.

Controlled Substances Act

In the United States, the Controlled Substances Act of 1970 became the basis for all later drug policy. The Act categorized drugs into five groups, according to how likely they were to be abused and how medicinally useful they were. Most countries now use a similar system. The Controlled Substances Act also created new federal agencies to combat drug use and trafficking. From that time, federal (as opposed to state and local) authorities took on a far greater role in the fight against recreational drug use. The U.S. Drug Enforcement Administration, established in 1973, also operates abroad.

The War on Drugs

In June 1971, U.S. President Richard Nixon made a speech in which he described substance abuse, or the use of illegal drugs, as "public enemy number one in the United States." He famously declared that America would wage a "War on Drugs".

The United States pursued the War on Drugs relentlessly. Other countries fought their own drug problems, but the U.S. effort was the most far-reaching. With its long borders and large, affluent population, the United States was the most tempting target for traffickers, and stopping the international drug business was a huge expensive.

As well as tough policing at home, at the borders, and on the high seas, the U.S. government took action abroad. Its goal was to cut off supplies from countries where drugs were produced or countries through which drugs were transported. The United States adopted a policy of cooperating with the governments of such countries, providing funds, advisers, and even special forces to help with law enforcement. Most of that activity was directed at the opium-producing regions of Central and South-East Asia and the coca-growing areas of South America.

Fighting the Opium Producers

In the 1990s, most of the world's opium was grown in two areas. The Central Asian "Golden Crescent" (Afghanistan, Pakistan, Iran) had a formidable rival in the Southeast Asian "Golden Triangle", a remote, mountainous area on the borders of Myanmar, Laos, and Thailand.

By the early 2000s, the Golden Triangle governments, with help from the United States, had largely stamped out opium production and trafficking. That was one of the great success stories of the U.S.

NARCO-TERRORISM

Narco-terrorism is a term used to describe terrorism funded by growing or dealing in drugs. In 2001, the United States and its allies overthrew the Taliban regime in Afghanistan, which sheltered terrorists. The Taliban have continued to resist capture, and finance their struggle by forcing farmers in the areas they control to produce opium. The Taliban make millions of dollars from the opium trade.

In Colombia, too, terrorists exploit the drug trade. Groups with different political ideas have fought one another and the government for more than 40 years. Several of the groups are thought to be involved in trafficking cocaine, notably FARC (Revolutionary Armed Forces of Colombia), which has carried out many successful kidnappings and other acts of terrorism.

An armed police guard stands by while a tractor uproots a poppy field in Afghanistan, the source of most of the world's supply of heroin.

drug policy. But with the loss of competition from the east, opium cultivation in Afghanistan increased rapidly. By 2008, Afghanistan produced 90 percent of the world's opium supply, amounting to more than 8,800 tons (7,983 tonnes) a year, most of it becoming heroin.

Fighting the Cocaine Producers

In South America, the war on drugs proved even harder to win. Farmers grew coca leaves in the mountainous regions of Colombia, Peru, and Bolivia. They then sold them to drug traffickers who processed the leaves into cocaine and smuggled the drug into the United States and other countries. The United States became involved in counter-narcotics activities in all three countries, funding and training Colombian government forces and assisting them in destoying coca crops.

PABLO ESCOBAR

The most famous of all drug traffickers, Pablo Escobar (1949–1993), was born in Rionegro, Colombia. At first a petty criminal, Escobar became a dealer in cocaine. He created an organization known as the Medellín Cartel, after his base, the Colombian city of Medellín. Escobar owed much of his success to his utter ruthlessness. Anyone who could not be bribed was murdered. His victims included judges, lawmakers, and police officials. The cartel smuggled vast quantities of drugs into the United States and other countries. By 1989, Escobar was thought to be the seventh richest man in the world. But his operations made him a target for rival gangs and Colombian and U.S. forces. In 1993, they tracked him down and killed him in a shoot-out at his Medellín hideout.

When this photograph was taken in 1989, Pablo Escobar was the head of the Medellín drug cartel in Colombia. Escobar became one of the richest and most feared men in the world. He was finally betrayed by rivals and killed in a gun battle in 1993.

During the 1970s and 1980s, the South American drug trade was dominated by Colombian cartels. Those criminal organizations became enormously powerful and violent. The U.S.-backed government forces began to make progress in 1993, when Pablo Escobar, head of the notorious Medellín Cartel, was shot dead. Within two years, other leaders of the Colombian cartels had been killed or sent to prison. Some were extradited, or sent to stand trial in another country (in this case, the United States).

That was a significant victory, but it did not end the drug problem. Traffickers reorganized and Mexican cartels took over important parts of the trade. When crops were destroyed in one area, traffickers used growers in a different place or even a different country. The poverty of farmers and the huge profits from trafficking meant that the drug trade seemed able to recover from even the most devastating blows. The war on drugs continued into the 2000s.

WHAT WOULD YOU DO?

You Are in Charge

You are the director of a drug enforcement agency. A very dangerous drug is entering your country from a neighboring nation where the government is not fully in control. What do you think will be the most effective way to combat the drug problem in your country? Why?

- You increase border patrol and customs officers to try to prevent drug smugglers from entering your country.

- You offer to help the neighboring country to train drug enforcement officers and advise its officials on strategy.

- You send your own law enforcement agents into the neighboring country to hunt down drug leaders and bring them to justice.

- You offer financial incentives and aid to farmers in that country to help them grow legal crops instead of drugs.

CHAPTER 6

Looking Ahead

It is 2025. Bruno is a doctor in Central Europe. He works in a clinic that treats people with drug problems. It is a very busy place, but well equipped and well funded. Thanks to improved medication and better counseling, getting over addiction is easier than it used to be. People must still want to give up drugs, but they have good reasons for doing so. It has become hard to obtain illegal drugs, and consequently they have become very expensive. A series of international agreements have made smuggling across borders very risky. Law enforcement agencies inside countries use very advanced technology that has helped them catch traffickers. With drug supplies running so low, using them and possibly becoming an addict seems like a bad idea. Drugs are no longer as desired by young people, who have become well informed of the risks associated with their use. Bruno thinks of his children Magda and Peter. He realizes that they are more aware of the dangers of drug use than he had been. He feels optimistic about their future.

Reports of Progress

Recent reports on drug trafficking have been favorable. The United Nations Office on Drugs and Crime (UNODC) issued a World Drug Report in 2007. It claimed that the 25-year-long rise in drug use had been halted, though worries remained about Afghanistan's soaring opium production. The United States' National Drug Threat Assessment for 2008 was similarly positive. Record drug seizures and strikes against traffickers had led to cocaine shortages in many cities. Methamphetamine production within the United States had fallen since 2004.

Some researchers disputed aspects of these claims. But on the whole it seemed that the situation had stabilized in the main markets of North America, Europe, Australia, and New Zealand. However, the reports also suggested that drug use was increasing in producer countries like Afghanistan, and also in transit regions such as Western Asia and West Africa.

The War on Drugs has not yet been won. And although stabilizing supply and use may be an achievement, existing problems are serious enough. The 2007 National Survey on Drug Use and Health estimated that 19.9 million Americans had used illegal drugs within the past month. That number includes 8 percent of Americans over eleven years old.

Iranian drug users prepare a heroin injection. Iran is a strict Islamic Republic where the use of recreational drugs is prohibited, yet there are increasing numbers of drug addicts. Drugs have taken hold in Iran, as they have in other countries on trafficking routes to the West.

WORLDWIDE SEIZURES OF SOME ILLEGAL DRUGS (IN POUNDS)

	1999	2000	2001	2002	2003	2004	2005
Heroin	79,871	118,492	119,226	107,008	117,379	132,718	129,191
Cocaine	811,076	754,953	822,558	819,130	1,099,977	1,277,358	1,658,537
Cannabis (Marijuana and Hashish)	8,911,925	10,305,010	10,708,450	10,460,478	12,897,651	13,645,177	18,999,438

Source: United Nations Office on Drugs and Crime, World Drug Reports, 2006 and 2007

International Cooperation

Even as the War on Drugs continues, advancements are often matched by setbacks. However, methods of detection and scanning keep improving and countries are working more closely with each other to combat trafficking. In May 2008, Iran, Pakistan, and Afghanistan agreed to strengthen border cooperation to stem the flow of drugs from Afghanistan. And in June 2008, the Merida Initiative committed the United States to spend $1.4 billion helping Mexico with law enforcement, training, and equipment.

Border Problems

At the same time, traffickers can also call on new resources. They cross the U.S. border, from north or south, in small private planes. Colombian traffickers have even used submarines to transport drugs. Border controls have been improved. However, the ever-increasing amount of drug traffic makes efficient checking very difficult. In Europe, goods and people pass more or less freely across borders within the 27-member European Union. Not having strict border control makes it harder to catch drug traffickers.

Recovering from drug addiction is extremely difficult. A former user comforts a heroin addict who has stopped injecting and is now suffering from very painful withdrawal symptoms.

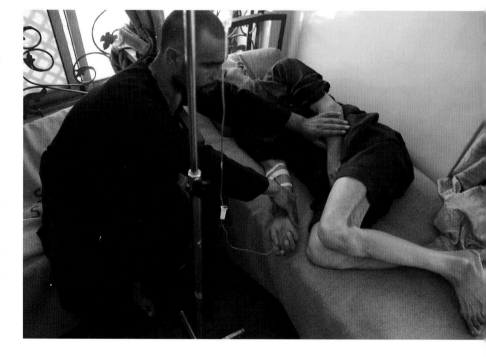

Prevention and Treatment

Most countries continue to fight against drug trafficking — the supply side of the trade. But recently there has been much more emphasis on prevention and treatment, championed by the United Nations.

U.N. policy reflects a belief that reducing the demand for drugs will benefit both individuals and society. Drug trafficking is so profitable that when one dealer is arrested, another dealer immediately takes over the business. If users stop wanting to buy drugs, however, the entire trade would collapse. Therefore, some governments are focusing on reducing demand by helping people overcome their addiction.

British studies suggest that a relatively small number of addicts commit a high proportion of all money-related crimes. When users were directed into treatment, there was a dramatic drop in the number of crimes they committed. Experts claimed that this was responsible for the 55 percent decrease in theft in the United Kingdom between 1997 and 2007.

In the United States, less attention has been given to drug prevention and treatment, including funding for education programs. Statistics show that U.S. spending on tough action against users, dealers, and international traffickers is increasing. In fact, it was growing at a much faster rate than spending on prevention and treatment (see chart below). The development of special U.S. drug courts from 1989 did, however, signal a willingness to understand individual offenders.

This chart compares the U.S. government's spending on the War on Drugs with its spending on drug treatment and prevention. The chart covers the period between 2002 and 2008.

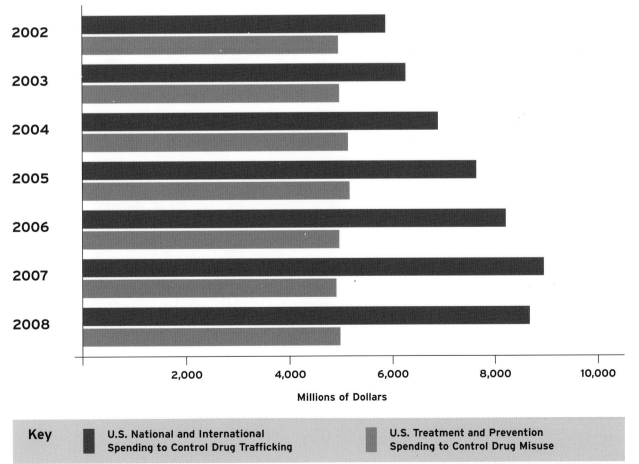

U.S. War on Drugs' Spending

Millions of Dollars

Key

U.S. National and International Spending to Control Drug Trafficking

U.S. Treatment and Prevention Spending to Control Drug Misuse

Source: National Drug Control Strategy, February 2009 Budget Summary

Harm Reduction

The United Nations is among the organizations that favor a principle known as harm reduction. That means trying to limit the damage done to and by users. For example, addicts' use of shared needles can spread diseases and they, in turn, may pass infections on to people who don't use drugs. The principle of harm reduction has led to some surprising initiatives. In 2001, Australia began to introduce injecting rooms where addicts could obtain and use clean needles. In 2005, addicts in several Canadian cities were issued with limited supplies of heroin to keep them out of trouble. Some critics have denounced such experiments, arguing that they make drug users feel that what they are doing is acceptable.

Different Approaches

There are other important differences between the way nations approach drug issues. The United States is notably tough on those who use drugs as well as those who sell them. Penalties vary according to circumstances, but are generally severe. The United States classifies drugs by dividing them into five groups, called schedules. Schedule 1 drugs are those that are highly likely to be

Australia's first injecting room, just after it opened in 2001. The medical director stands in the facility, where addicts can inject in hygienic conditions.

abused and are considered to have no medical use. Those include heroin, LSD, marijuana, and ecstasy. Schedule 2 drugs, such as cocaine, methamphetamine, amphetamines, and morphine, are also liable to abuse but have limited medical uses. Schedule 3 drugs, which include barbiturates and steroids, have less potential for abuse and more widely accepted medical uses.

The British approach is broadly similar to that of the United States, though its classification system is slightly different (see panel).

CLASSIFIED DRUGS IN THE UNITED KINGDOM

In the United Kingdom, drugs are officially grouped into three classes: A, B, and C. That classification reflects the harm that experts believe the drug can do. The most severe penalties are reserved for the most harmful drugs, or Class A. As in most countries, selling drugs is more severely punished than possession or use of drugs.

Class	Some Classified Drugs	Penalties for Possession	Penalties for Selling/Dealing
A	heroin, cocaine, crack, LSD, ecstasy, crystal meth, magic mushrooms	up to 7 years in prison or unlimited fine; or both	up to life in prison or unlimited fine; or both
B	amphetamines, cannabis,* Ritalin	up to 5 years in prison or unlimited fine; or both	up to 14 years in prison or unlimited fine; or both
C	tranquilizers, ketamine, some painkillers	up to 2 years in prison	up to 14 years in prison or unlimited fine; or both

*reclassified from C to B from 2009

Source: www.homeoffice.gov.uk/drugs/drugs-law

A number of European countries have a different approach. Portugal punishes drug dealing, but since 2001 it has treated drug abuse and addiction as a medical problem rather than a crime. When a user is found in possession of drugs, they are confiscated. The drug user is examined by a health and welfare commission, which decides on an appropriate medical treatment.

DRUG EPIDEMIC

From the 1990s, a little-known drug became disturbingly popular in the United States, Australia, and New Zealand. Methamphetamine, a concentrated and dangerous form of amphetamine, is better known as crystal meth. Anyone using crystal meth experiences an intense high, four times stronger than the high from cocaine. But the side effects such as, exhaustion, addiction, and mental deterioration, are equally extreme and happen quickly. An important ingredient of crystal meth is pseudophedrine, which is found in a number of cold medicines. The United States' 2005 Combat Methamphetamine Epidemic Act allowed people to buy pseudophedrine only after the closest of checks. By 2007, the British authorities had also become concerned about increasing use of crystal meth, and they changed its status to a Class A drug.

This child is being cuddled by his new sister. He has been adopted by a foster family after being neglected by his own parents, who were crystal meth addicts. Such children often have serious health problems.

Decriminalizing Marijuana

Many countries have laws against possessing marijuana but do not enforce them vigorously. That drug has less serious effects than heroin and cocaine. That is one reason why Belgium and Switzerland have decided not to regard possession of cannabis as a crime. Users who possess small amounts are not charged with any wrongdoing.

The Netherlands has launched the most radical policy experiment so far. The policy strongly emphasizes harm reduction. Possessing small amounts of cannabis for personal use is not a criminal offense. Most controversially, many adult-only cafés sell small amounts of cannabis (5 grams, which is less than one ounce), which users can smoke on the premises. The Dutch policy has been widely criticized by European neighbors and others, who believe that treating cannabis smoking as an ordinary activity is misguided.

Changing Attitudes

Even in Europe, the trend to treat drug users as serious offenders is gaining momentum. Governments change, and policies change with them. In 2006, a newly elected Italian government introduced laws that replaced a mild attitude toward drug possession with very stiff penalties. Political pressures, new evidence, new treatments, and new strains of known drugs can all affect existing government policies.

Different approaches to outlawing drug problems have different advantages. Over time, some policies show better results than others. When they do, governments should gradually adopt them and further progress can be expected. A world free of illegal drugs may be unrealistic, but it is possible to create a world in which drugs no longer ruin thousands of lives and threaten the health of societies.

WHAT WOULD YOU DO?

You Are in Charge

Your school has never had any serious problem with drugs, but now there are rumors that a student is selling drugs on the premises. As class president, you support a decision to:

■ Search students and their lockers for drugs or drug paraphernalia.

■ Conduct random drug tests on students.

■ Start a counseling service to help young people who may be tempted by drugs or have existing drug problems.

■ Put up posters warning students of the dangers of drugs that explain where they can get help for drug problems or addiction.

■ Start a tip line, so students can report drug dealing to authorities anonymously.

Glossary

addiction A condition in which a person finds it almost impossible to stop using a drug, even when it is obviously harming him or her

AIDS See HIV/AIDS

bust A police arrest, especially one that nets many criminals and breaks up their organization

caffeine The drug present in coffee, tea, chocolate, and many soft drinks

coca The South American plant from which cocaine is made

dealer A person who sells drugs

dependence Another word for addiction

drug baron A top criminal who runs a drug-dealing network

extradite When a person is extradited, he or she is removed from a country, with the permission of that country's government, to stand trial in a different country

gateway drug A drug thats use is believed by some people to lead to the use of more harmful drugs

hallucinogen A drug that distorts the user's sense of reality, producing hallucinations

hard drug A drug that has visibly serious, negative effects on users

hepatitis C A disease of the liver

HIV/AIDS HIV (human immunodeficiency virus) is a virus that destroys the immune system. People whose infections resulting from HIV have become life-threatening are described as having AIDS (acquired immunodeficiency syndrome).

hypodermic syringe A medical instrument for giving injections, also used by drug users

mule A person paid to carry drugs through foreign checkpoints

narco-terrorism Drug terrorism funded by the profits from growing or dealing in drugs

narcotics Illegal drugs

nicotine The drug in cigarettes that makes it hard for a regular smoker to quit smoking

opiate A depressant drug made from the opium poppy such as codeine, morphine, and opium

overdose Excessive drug use that takes place on a single occasion, with life-threatening or fatal results

peer pressure The pressure to behave like other members of a group, especially among young people

pharmaceutical To do with medicines and drugs

rehabilitation The process by which a drug user is able to become a normally functioning member of the community

sedative A drug that makes the user relaxed or drowsy; a depressant

soft drug A drug that has a milder effect and is less harmful than hard drugs, such as heroin or cocaine

solvent One of many common products, such as glue, that can be used like a drug, typically by sniffing its vapors

steroids Drugs that build up the muscles and improve athletic performance

stimulant A drug that gives the user a sense of being more alive, making him or her feel more energetic and confident

Further Information

Books

Bauder, Julia. *Drug Trafficking.* (Greenhaven Press, 2007)

Donnellan, Craig. *Issues: Drug Abuse* (Independence Educational Publishers, 2006)

Fooks, Louie. *Twenty-First Century Debates: The Drugs Trade* (Wayland, 2003)

Landau, Elaine. Meth: America's Drug Epidemic. (Twenty-First Century Books, 2007)

McGuigan, Jim. *Just the Facts: The Drugs Trade* (Heinemann, 2005)

Smith, A. *In the News: Drug Culture* (Franklin Watts, 2003)

Web Sites

Freevibe.com
www.freevibe.com
Review this interactive web site that investigates the risks of drug taking and includes young peoples' stories.

National Institute of Drug Abuse (NIDA)
teens.drugabuse.gov
This official U.S. government web site provides information on a wide range of drugs and includes a glossary, facts, personal stories, and FAQs.

U.S. Drug Enforcement Administration
www.usdoj.gov/dea/index.htm
The U.S. DEA web site offers national news updates about the War on Drugs and information about current U.S. drug laws and policies.

U.N. Global Youth Network
www.unodc.org/youthnet
This U.N. web site for teens offers news about drug topics involving young people from all over the world.

Publisher's note to educators and parents: Our editors have carefully reviewed these web sites to ensure that they are suitable for children. Many web sites change frequently, however, and we cannot guarentee that a site's future contents will continue to meet our high standards of quality and educational value. Be advised that children should be closely supervised whenever they access the Internet.

What Would You Do?

Page 11:
You may consider refusing because some of your admirers will think you are being uncool. But the issue is important and you are in a good position to help prevent drug abuse. Since you are probably not an expert on drugs, you will be taken most seriously if you stick to the area you know about. You can almost certainly speak with authority about cases of performance-enhancing drugs in sports which have come to light in recent years. You can wholeheartedly condemn that kind of drug use, which endangers health, is basically a form of cheating, and ends the careers of those who are caught.

Page 19:
If you are a good president, you will try to look after all people. You will not want farmers to suffer, so you will keep direct action against them to a minimum. In any case, if only drug crops offer farmers a decent living, they will probably plant them again once the police or army have gone. Patroling the borders and cooperating with neighboring states will, if effective, certainly discourage traffickers. But the only long-term solution is to make it worthwhile for farmers to stop cultivating drug crops and grow other crops instead. That is easier said than done. Rewarding farmers for harvesting alternative crops will make it easier for them to change, but sooner or later the new crops will have to pay for themselves. Plans involving irrigation and fertilizers are more useful in the long run, since they improve the quality and size of the harvest.

Page 23:
Those questions are well worth debating, though there are no clear answers. Most people would like to see more effective policing, but increased police powers have less support. In democracies, people value their rights and want to limit the power of governments and police to interfere with them. You may approve of targeting hard rather than soft drugs if you accept that there are significant differences between them. Your decision may also depend on whether you believe that using soft drugs leads to the use of hard ones. Few people would question the value of educational and rehabilitation programs. Since prisons are already overcrowded, there are advantages to sending offenders to rehabilitation rather than jailing them.

Page 29:
You may be tempted to concentrate resources on people whose sickness seems to be the result of bad luck rather than self-harming behavior. However, not everyone would agree that all drug addicts are to blame for their condition and, without help, they could continue to spread the disease to others. Providing drug addicts with equipment they need to inject drugs is a controversial idea, but it is a practical way to help stop blood-borne diseases from spreading. Offering free medical treatment is an incentive that may encourage some addicts to get help for their addiction. However, it won't work unless those users are personally committed to quitting their drug habits.

Page 37:
Tightening border security is a good start but it is impossible to completely seal off a country's borders. Drug traffickers have ingenious ways of getting their products to foreign markets. As drug trafficking is an international problem, it makes sense to work cooperatively with other governments, particularly in countries that are known for producing drugs. Poorer countries may need assistance to train police in drug enforcement. Sending your own drug enforcement agents into a foreign country is risky, and should only be done with the permission and cooperation of the foreign government. Using your funds to give direct assistance to farmers who grow drug crops may help eliminate those crops, but if farmers remain poor, they will probably return to growing illegal drug crops.

Page 45:
Your school has been drug free, so there is a good case for moving cautiously in a rumor-based situation. Searching students and testing for drugs may well create a tense, unpleasant atmosphere. In the United States, drug testing is used only for out-of-school activities. You may set up some form of counseling in the school, but students are often reluctant to discuss sensitive matters among their peers. Redirecting them to anonymous telephone helplines is a good alternative. That outlet would enable students to alert authorities without having to give their name. In a school setting, educating students about the health risks associated with drug use and the dangers of dealing drugs is appropriate.

Index

Page numbers in **bold** refer to illustrations and charts.

About the Author

Nathaniel Harris was born in London and educated at University College, Oxford. He taught and worked in publishing before becoming a full-time writer. He has written many books on modern history.